THE GOOD LIFE ALBUM OF HELEN & SCOTT NEARING

The Samuel Grinspoons

The GOOD LIFE Album

of HELEN & SCOTT NEARING

by Helen Nearing

A Chatham Book

Sunrise Books/E.P. Dutton & Co., Inc.

TO SCOTT,
who is more at ease
with facts than photographs.

Published simultaneously in Canada by Clarke, Irwin & Company
Limited, Toronto and Vancouver
ISBN: 0-87690-144-5
Library of Congress Catalog Number: 74-81421

Dutton-Sunrise Inc.,
a subsidiary of E.P. Dutton & Co., Inc.

PHOTOGRAPHIC NOTE: In all cases photographs
have been credited to the photographer if known. When no
credit appears with an illustration, it is because the
identity of the photographer could not be established.

CONTENTS

Scott and I at ease in the kitchen of the farmhouse at Forest Farm in Harborside, Maine. Dried herbs and vegetables hang overhead for our use when they aren't available fresh from our garden.

INTRODUCTION

SCOTT AND I, in our similar and dissimilar ways, have each had a vision of the good life. We have been fortunate enough to be able to work at it together for more than four decades. Whether this is sufficient reason to write and talk about it we do not know. The important thing is: we try to live it.

Christopher Harris, the publisher of this volume, and Lotte Jacobi, whose idea it was, wanted a pictorial record of the life we have led together and the steps leading to its achievement. The accompanying photographs give a backward glance at us from crabbed old age to babyhood.

One picture is said to be worth a thousand words. We have tended, up to now, to deal in words rather than pictures. In fact, we have written more than a thousand words for every photograph we have taken. Nevertheless, many pictures have been taken of us through the years, which I have collected here to illustrate the joint and separate lives we have lived from 1883 to 1974.

We have enjoyed the years of our good life together and hope some of it shines through. We gladly share what we know and what we do with any interested person, especially the growing numbers of young people who are now engaged in homesteading. This book is one of our efforts in that direction.

I believe Scott was always an advocate and practitioner of the good life. Everything I have heard or read about him before I met him indicates that his sense of truth, justice and integrity were highly developed from childhood on through adolescence and young manhood. All I have come to know about him since reaffirms that conviction.

In Philadelphia, at the University of Pennsylvania, Scott put seven years of undergraduate and graduate work into economics, sociology, political science, education and history. Then he started to teach in his Alma Mater. He spoke in and out of the classroom against discrimination, poverty and exploitation. He not only protested against the evils of the social situation but he advocated certain changes in the social pattern which would, he believed, bring an end to the inequities and injustices which he saw around him.

Matters came to a head in 1914-17 during the general blood bath of that period. Scott lost four good academic jobs in rapid succession, was excluded from the lecture platform and was eased off magazine pages to which he had been contributing rather extensively. He saw his text books taken from the schools, was indicted by a Federal Grand Jury on the charge that his pamphlet, *The Great Madness,* by analyzing the causes of the war as commercial, obstructed recruiting and enlistment in the armed forces. Though he was tried and acquitted by a jury of his peers, from then on he was blacklisted by the academic world and ostracized by the shapers of public opinion. Consequently, he could not teach, speak, write or print through the established channels of communication.

Scott stood at the crossroads: should he give up the struggle, climb on the bandwagon, ask forgiveness of the Powers That Be and promise thereafter to serve and applaud the social system to which he was opposed? Or should he start a new life and redouble his efforts to oppose the inequities of the system?[1] At about that time I met him.

My middle-class background was similar to Scott's in many ways but my path in life had been a far easier one. My home life in Ridgewood, New Jersey was happy, comfortable and well-adjusted. My parents, who met when my mother was an art student visiting this country from her native Holland, were intellectuals interested and active in civic affairs: President of the Board of Education and the local Red Cross; President of the Woman's Club and the local Society for Prevention of Cruelty to Animals, etc.

My father, a New York businessman, was especially fond of music, had a fine tenor voice and was delighted when I showed aptitude in this direction. Violin lessons started early, and immediately after graduating from Ridgewood High School I went to Europe to continue my musical studies. In Amsterdam and Vienna I found teachers of note.

Contact with Mrs. Annie Besant (the President of the Theosophical Society with headquarters in Adyar, Madras) and Krishnamurti and his brother Nityananda led me from a paramount interest in music to the study of Eastern religions and Theosophy. I went with them to India in the early 1920's and from there to Australia where I lived for several years in a community on Sydney Harbor which would now be called a commune. This was a particularly happy period of "spiritual" education in Raja Yoga (not Hatha Yoga), meditation and music making, in congenial surroundings with other young people.

I returned to the United States after years abroad, with my head in the clouds and with no knowledge of what had been going on in the world. I had hardly done a stroke

---

[1] He has told the story of this dilemma in his political autobiography *The Making of a Radical.* New York: Harper & Row, 1972

of work in my life and had lived generally as a parasite. I was a complete political ignoramus.

I met Scott in Ridgewood where he also lived at the time and there started my real-life education. To get me in touch with reality he urged a stint of factory work. I surely needed to get down to earth and see how the other half lived. I took jobs at minimum wages, starting with candy packing at $11 a week and living in a $7-a-week hall bedroom in Brooklyn. I went on to other jobs and eventually to a box factory on West 14th Street in New York where I folded and glued for a skimpy $13 a week. When I asked for more wages I was fired. One of my jobs there was to sweep under the machines before leaving for the day. When I held the broom handle tight under my right arm while I swept, the girls laughed at me: "looks as if you never held a broom before." Little did they know that that was the truth.

Scott was at a particularly low ebb when I met him in 1930. He had no paying work at the time and had just been expelled from the Communist Party on grounds of insubordination for having published a book on imperialism of which the Party disapproved. He was not allowed to speak or write or teach in any quarter. We were exceedingly poor and lived in a three-room cold-water unheated (except for a small wood stove) flat on Avenue C and 14th Street, New York, for which we paid a royal $20 a month. We decided we would rather be poor in the country than poor in the city so, in 1932, we moved to a rundown old farm in southern Vermont, for which we paid $300 down and took on an $800 mortgage.

Imagine the distress of my parents when I first left music for supernal relations with Krishnamurti and then bumped to the gritty ground with Scott Nearing. However, after Scott and I were settled in Vermont, they came to see the stability and purpose of our homesteading venture, and knowing I had not completely abandoned the fiddle, became reconciled and learned to respect and to love Scott.

We were convinced that life could be good and were determined to make ours so. We were prepared to spend the time, energy and persistence necessary, even if that meant a rather complete estrangement from civilization. Born and brought up in the richest nation on earth, with its multitudinous gadgets and gimcracks as part and parcel of our daily lives, we realized that we must be prepared to reject these toys, to strike out for ourselves and to pioneer in the real sense of that term.

After considering possibilities in Europe and various parts of North America we chose to live in New England, because the changing seasonal climate seemed congenial to us, its society less solidly hostile, economic costs more moderate, and because the tradition of pioneering and of individualism was still alive there.

Our sojourn in New England has divided itself into two parts: nineteen years in Vermont, in what then was a mountain wilderness at the north base of Stratton Mountain, and twenty-two years at saltwater level on Penobscot Bay in coastal Maine.

The shift to Maine was unavoidable for us. The threat and finally the conversion of the Stratton Mountain wilderness and its vicinity into one of the most sophisticated and manicured ski areas of the East gave us no choice. The corruption and spoilation of the countryside was accompanied by a disastrous explosion in the cost of everything from taxes and land to mittens and maple syrup.

We have written about the Vermont experience in some detail in *Living the Good Life*[2] and *The Maple Sugar Book*.[3] There we were able to try out various aspects of subsistence living and to convince ourselves that pioneering in 20th-century New England was a real possibility, replete with many deep satisfactions.

We had taken over a badly eroded, exhausted farm in a denuded valley. Scott and I planned the project carefully, built a house and several outbuildings of native stone, turned a piece of depleted soil into a productive garden, built up a source of cash income from maple sugaring and made the entire project into a going, self-supporting concern. We are convinced that anyone who really wants to can follow suit by selecting a site, outlining a program and sticking to it until it has produced results. The experience will be educative, health-giving, exciting, even inspiring.

Will such a move solve the outstanding social problems? Certainly not. Is it a cure-all for the ills which beset modern man? Far from it. For us, it proved to be a means of steadying and stabilizing one household in a teetery world and of providing the members of that household with an economic base from which they could make their leisure time contribute toward the advancement of the general welfare.

Not everyone would be willing to follow suit. After talking to and watching thousands of visitors to both our farms it is clear that most people prefer to stay with the crowd, pushing buttons, growing pale, drawn and ulcered. They find it easier, less painful, to be led even to the bank teller's cage or the killing pen than to leave the rut and strike out on a new and independent path.

Certain requirements are necessary before one branches out or tackles an experiment of this nature. You have to have a place on which to experiment. You have to have a minimum of capital to pay for land, buildings and tools. You have to be able to plan and to follow through. Determination and persistence are necessary. You have to learn to be your own gardener, mower, woodsman, architect, builder, carpenter, mason, mechanic,

[2] New York: Schocken Books, 1970
[3] New York: John Day, 1950. Reprinted in 1971 by Schocken Books, New York.

repairman, cook and general improviser. You have to have much initiative and aplomb.

Vermont was a beautiful unspoiled state when we lived there in the 1930's and 1940's. When the ski industry and summer tourists threatened to engulf the whole state and particularly our quiet valley, rather than adapt and change our values, we left. With our Vermont experience as a useful background, we moved to Maine during the early spring of 1952. A short week of search in the autumn of 1951 had led us to a remote cove along the Maine seacoast between Castine and Deer Isle where we found a derelict one-hundred-forty-acre farm situated on Cape Rosier. The widowed owner was anxious to sell because the place was too isolated and lonely, a condition which happened to suit our purposes exactly.

On this second Forest Farm, in Maine, we have again put down our roots into the good earth. We had learned the inestimable value of rootedness during our apprentice-ship to organic agriculture in the narrow valleys and on the steep hills of the Green Mountains. This lesson was just as valid on the rugged shores of Penobscot Bay.

In Maine as in Vermont we made serious and various attempts to live at five levels: with nature; by doing our daily stint of bread labor; by carrying on our professional activities; by constant association with our fellow citizens; and by unremitting efforts to cultivate the life of the mind and spirit.

We again were setting up and carrying on a largely self-supporting homestead based upon a use economy. As vegetarians, we raised our own food, ate it and enjoyed excellent health. We cut our own firewood, cooked and heated with it. We built up the top soil by adding compost and other organic matter, drained and filled in swamps, dug a pond, thinned and weeded our wood lot, clearing some additional acres from which we could cut hay, and built a sun-heated greenhouse which extended our season of garden greens by several months. We added to our buildings. (At the moment of writing, in our 70's and 90's, we are working at two fairly large stone buildings down by the water-side. We hope to have them finished by 1976.)

We have organized and incorporated a Social Science Institute, chartered to do non-profit educational work. We research, publish and distribute literature in the social science field; take every opportunity to speak or write on matters of general educational interest; take part in the development of arts and crafts. We maintain a good library and share it with those who are interested in our field. We subscribe to innumerable magazines and papers and belong to many forward-looking organizations. All this we call our professional activities.

We early established real friendships with many of the Maine natives and were made to feel at home. We take an active part in their agricultural and educational activities.

We have spoken at dozens of meetings at schools, colleges, churches and other local groups on "the Good Life" and its widespread implications. The State-appointed Commission on the Arts and Humanities, in January 1971, selected Scott along with five other citizens for an award "to those whose life and work have brought special distinction to our state," citing him for "making an art of his life." "Scott Nearing," wrote Governor Curtis in his citation, "has lived in Maine since 1952 on a saltwater farm that looks out upon Penobscot Bay, a farm that he and his like-minded wife, Helen, have returned, by bread labor, to bountiful production. There the doors are open to the hundreds of people of all ages who come each year to learn the secrets of living off the land, and yet, within that rigorous discipline, finding the energy and leisure for writing, for music, for civic affairs. Long before many of us were born, this man was doing battle. He spoke out against child labor, against war; he predicted the decay of great cities, the pollution of air and waters, the decline of personal independence. Economist, environmentalist, sociologist, lecturer and writer, he prescribed the Good Life and practiced what he preached." Our roots in Maine had become educational and social as well as agricultural and economic.

We make special efforts to help in organizing local and regional projects that can raise cultural awareness. We take an active interest in all efforts to establish and maintain peace on the planet. We travel, when we can, to the East and to the West, in our own country and in Asia and Europe.

We encourage and help those who are planning to build their own subsistence homesteads. We know personally hundreds of young people who are either completing their academic careers or dropping out of educational institutions and looking about for a place to live and work. To the thousands who come to see us, we are glad to show our enterprises and experiments. We are happy to make suggestions to those starting out with plenty of aspiration and hope, but little of the concrete experience and knowledge which are the ripe products of planned, thoughtful, purposeful living.

As I read over what I've written above, it all seems like a tall order for two ordinary members of the human family. Yet it's been no great strain for us. Undoubtedly, amicable and congenial relations between the two of us have helped through the years. Our ideas and ideals deep down are the same. Our attitudes to life are the same—to nature, to animals, to plants, to country living, to simplicity, to quietude, and to the cosmos in general.

We are extremely lucky to have shared a good life together.

Forest Farm, Harborside, Maine
May, 1974

HELEN K. NEARING

MAINE

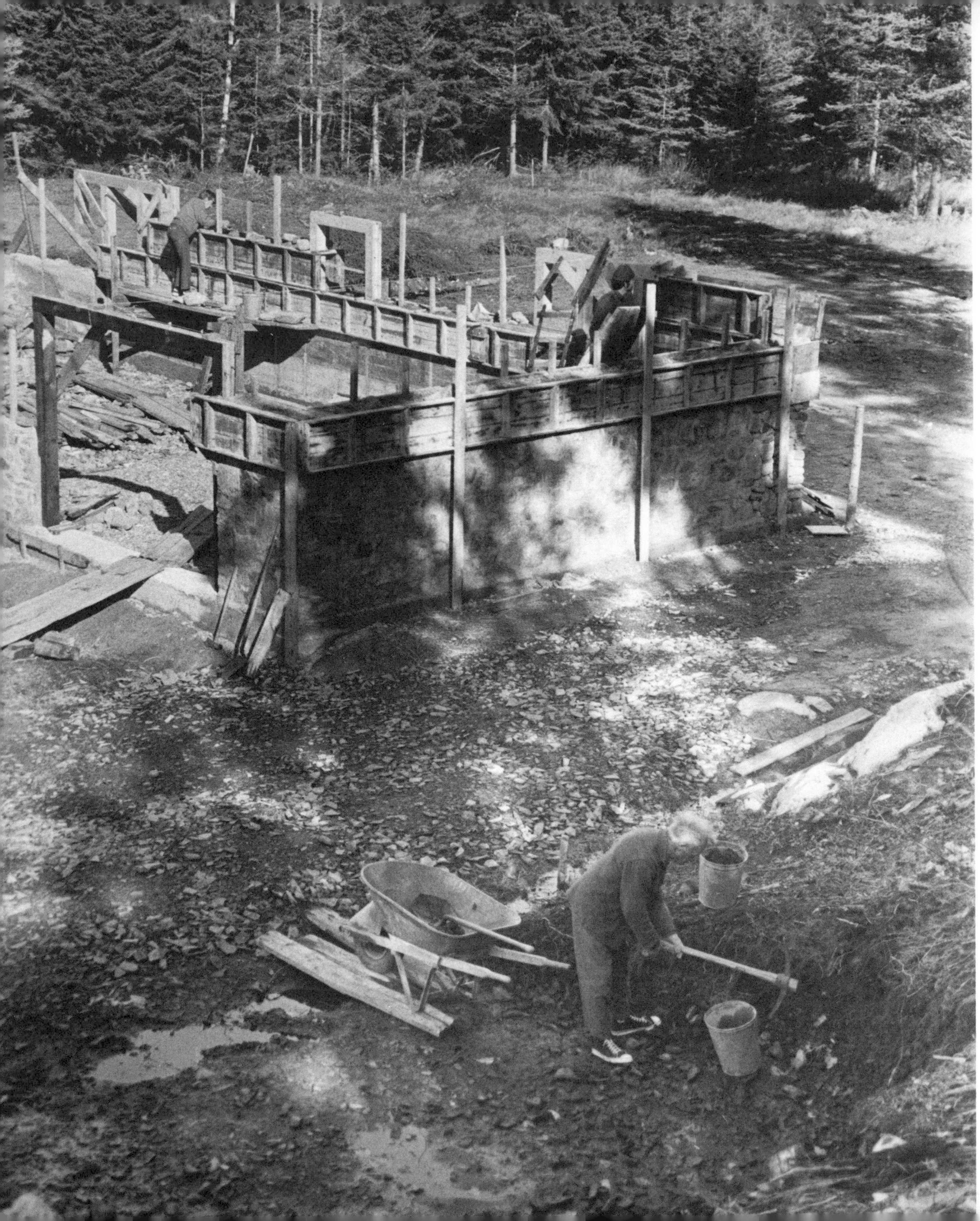

Christopher Harris

Leland Witting

Christopher Harris

Leland Witting

We are building a new stone house in Maine, down by the waterside. Here we are putting up a garage-workshop in the fall and early winter of 1973. We are employing the same techniques, and the same wooden forms, we used in Vermont in the 1930's.

Christopher Harris

16

Soil improvement for the vegetable gardens, fruit trees, berry bushes and flowers requires regular organic composting and mulching. Scott's compost piles are above. At the left, we both gather seaweed by the cove on Penobscot Bay for mulching material.

18

At right is the pond behind the farmhouse in Maine, created by Scott who dug and removed 15,000 wheelbarrow loads of sod, topsoil and muck in the process. Below is our woodshed with green firewood stacked like a teepee for drying.

Christopher Harris

Richard Garrett

Our sun-heated greenhouse, in which we start and grow a lot of our food before, during and after the outdoor growing season. Opposite are some flats of lettuce in varying stages of growth, photographed in the greenhouse in November.

I am here about to enter the walled vegetable garden (100 x 100 feet) where Scott is moving something around in the wheelbarrow.

Scott receiving gifts and tributes, including the Friends of Nature award, on his 90th birthday, in 1973.

Richard Garrett

Richard Garrett

Richard Garrett

Scott at work on the many regular chores around our fifty-acre Forest Farm in Maine. The property, originally 140 acres, purchased from Mary Stackhouse in 1952, has required systematic attention to convert it from briars and thicket to a productive homestead farm.

Scott and I harvesting various crops:
Opposite, Scott with a bouquet of our
famous sweet peas; above, I reach for pea
pods from a stepladder; above right, for
raspberries; and right, for fresh corn.

Richard Garret

The vegetable garden (above) was walled in to keep out the deer and other hungry creatures. Using the stonework technique developed in Vermont, Scott and I built the whole thing (opposite) from stones gathered around the farm and down by the beach.

Overleaf is a comprehensive midsummer view of our farmhouse and sheds from across the garden and the roof of the greenhouse.

Richard Garrett

At left, I am bringing an armload of lettuce towards the kitchen. Below, Scott spreads onions out on planks in the field to dry for winter use. Opposite, above, are some of our own preserves in the cellar of the house. Jams, tomato juice, rosehip juice, raspberry juice, applesauce and soup stock occupy these shelves. Opposite, below, the two of us share lunch set out on the stone patio by the kitchen door.

Gilbert E. Friedberg

33

Above, Pusso, one of a series of Maine cats, at the kitchen window. At right, a sequence beginning at the top shows Scott blowing with his special copper pipe on the coals in the kitchen stove to get the wood fire going, followed by me at work with pots and pans, and Scott enjoying the results at the evening meal.

34

Gilbert E. Friedberg   *Christopher Harris*

Above, an important focal point on the library wall, a plaster cast made by an artist friend of my father's. At right, a kitchen window with the usual accumulation of tools, flowers and knickknacks.

Richard Garrett

Soup for lunch (opposite) is usual fare. We eat almost everything out of wooden bowls, and with wooden spoons or chopsticks.

Above, Scott inspects drill bits which belonged to his grandfather. Because we believe tools deserve care and respect, these bits still remain in fine condition after more than a century of use.

Richard Garrett

Richard Garrett

A great many visitors, both old friends and strangers, come to Forest Farm regularly. Above, left, neighbors listen to an outdoor talk by Scott. Above, right, I sort through pictures with Lotte Jacobi and Anne Harris for this book. Below, right, Scott autographs a book for an admirer while I admire the admirer. On the opposite page, Scott appears to be the listener from his favorite chair in the kitchen.

Opposite: the kitchen door and the beginnings of an outdoor meal.
Above is such a typical meal in full swing. Visitors, helpers and friends
(anywhere up to 30 per day) are almost always on hand.

At left, Scott discusses the growing of vegetables with a group of visitors in the garden. Above, I share a rock in the cove with Whitey, the cat that came with the farm.

43

Richard Garrett

At left and opposite is a scarecrow lady I made up in 1968 for a Garden Club show. One of Scott's great grandchildren offers the lady a duck. Below are some Japanese from a Surrey music school who came to a party we gave them on Hiroshima Day.

44

46

The winter of 1956 included my skating on the pond behind
the house and plenty of beautiful snow.

Summer scenes from the 1950's, including two views of Penobscot Bay. Spirit Cove, left and opposite, is in front of Forest Farm. Below is Whitey, the cat, perched on me, and Blacky, another one of my favorites, perched on a stack of newspapers.

48

The present Pusso stands guard inside the kitchen door.

VERMONT

The snowbound main house of our first Forest Farm.

Above, I am about to enter the front door of Forest Farm in Jamaica, Vermont, and below, I am with Scott and author Richard Gregg, in 1951.

The early spring view over the Forest Farm rooftops to Stratton Mountain.

Scott performs on the recorder while I listen critically.

Many Sunday mornings were devoted to sing-song gatherings on the back patio. Opposite, I am caught entranced with the music. Above, Scott joins in with Norm Williams, Alfred Jacobs and others. At right, I am singing with Scott's granddaughter Elka, Natalie Field and Lois Smith. Below, Pearl Buck and her husband, Richard Walsh, join a session.

Irene Straus

Above, a group of snowy Vermont neighbors with Scott in 1949. Below, my mother and I on top of Vermont's Mount Equinox in October of 1951. Opposite, Scott and I converse on the Forest Farm stone patio, also in 1951.

Maple sugaring was an important source of livelihood for us in Vermont. Left, I am collecting sap in 1940. Below, Scott and I walk off through the sugarbush. Opposite are our two sugarhouses and two settling tanks. Below that, I hitch a ride on the back of a sled bound for collecting firewood.

58

Left, the sugarhouse steaming away, surrounded by the season's supply of firewood. Below, a neighbor's team of oxen which helped us in 1935, the first year we sugared. Below, left, fellow workers haul in wood to fuel the evaporator.

Irene Strauss

Opposite, I am at work stoking the 5 x 15 foot evaporator.

FOREST FARMS

MAPLE SYRUP

MAPLE CANDY

Llewellyn Ransom

Opposite, I pose with the mail by our sign at the end of the driveway. At right, Scott cooks maple sugar on the kitchen stove while, below, I pour the hot sugar into rubber candy molds. At bottom right, Scott and I pack cans of syrup for shipping.

Irene Strauss

Irene Strauss

In addition to making maple sugar, we wrote about it too. Above, I pack up a copy of our book for mailing. Opposite, at a sugaring-off party in New York, I am joined by hungry officials of the Vermont Sugar Makers' Association. Our book is prominently displayed while Scott stays nearly out of sight behind us.

We put up eight stone buildings in Vermont, one log cabin, one concrete guest cabin, two galvanized sugarhouses and two woodsheds. Above, I examine the ledge on which we built a study in the woods for Scott. At right, the study in the process of construction and, below, the finished product. Opposite, Scott mixes concrete by shovel in a wheelbarrow.

The biggest project was the main house we built for ourselves on the property we bought in 1934 from Mercy Hoard. Opposite, above, is the boulder photographed in 1940, against which we built the house and which became the back wall of the living room. Below, the construction begins. In the far left picture, I am caught dreaming on top of our boulder, while on the right, I am at work laying up the stone fireplace. Above, at the left, is a later stage in the construction, in 1941, and at the right, I am in the completed living room with the great boulder wall visible in the background.

We were always building. Above, I am joined by our neighbor, Jack Lightfoot, pointing the stonework on the wall of the garage. At right is the hand-turned cement mixer, and below is the view towards Pinnacle Mountain from the sand-pit site of the stone cottage we built together in 1938.

At right, nearly finished, is the three-room cottage facing Pinnacle. Below is one of our open-air woodsheds, and to the right of that is the first stone cabin we built in Vermont.

Above is our garden on the hill in Vermont with raspberries, asparagus and other vegetables. At right, Scott builds up the compost pile with clumps of sod.

72

Scott and Jack Lightfoot break ground
with Jack's two horse-power plow.

73

At work in the garden. Here, from top to bottom, I am sowing seeds, planting seedlings, and putting in brush on which the pea vines still climb. Opposite, I am being helped by my niece, Barbara Vaughan, in picking the peas which have obviously flourished.

At left, Scott and I visit Sunset Hill, the highest point at Forest Farm. Below, we eat a meal, in 1940, behind the original farmhouse which we bought from the Ellonens in the fall of 1932.

76

Scott, writing at the kitchen table.

Above, Scott and I sunbathing and fluting by the pool behind the first stone cabin. At right, I play my fiddle for a country dance at Pikes Falls, Vermont.

Opposite, I'm coming home from a morning on skis. Above, left, Scott and I pose in 1942 with our first automobile, a Dodge pick-up truck. At the right is the back door of the old Ellonen house, our first home in Vermont.

Above is the first stonework we did—a living room added onto the side of the original Ellonen house in 1934. Opposite, above, is the stone fireplace we built in the new living room. Below is the nearest store to our farm in 1941, in Bondville, Vermont.

Overleaf is the Ellonen house, with the stone addition at the left. Scott removes a heavy accumulation of snow from the driveway.

Surrounded with tools for woodcutting, I recline
for a moment in the spring of 1934.

At right, neighboring cows pass by our mailbox on the Pikes Falls road. Below, Scott and I head uphill with a pole to support our grapevines.

85

Above, Scott and a truckload of my family in 1933: my sister, Alice Vaughan, and her daughter, Barbara, and my parents. Below, Scott and I with shorn hair (we shaved it to the bone that summer) on the front steps of the Ellonen house. Beside me is my mother, while Scott's lecture manager, Roxanna Wells, occupies a chair on the porch. Opposite is the Ellonen farmhouse in its original state when we first bought it in 1931.

Another gathering by the Ellonen house. Scott (rear, left) and I (extreme right), with hair still on, join my parents, sister and niece, plus Maria and Josef Sonnweber, old friends from Ehrwald, Tirol.

OUT IN THE WORLD

Scott, who looks asleep, being sculpted by Zena Posever in Miami: March, 1961.

Joe Goldstein

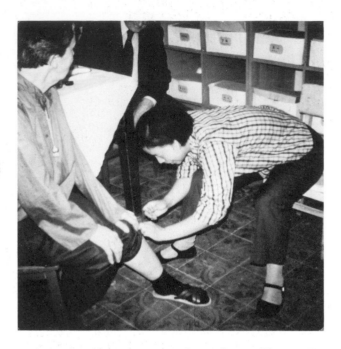

Above, two snapshots taken in China in June of 1973. At left, I receive impromptu acupuncture treatment in a Shanghai clinic. On the right, Scott and Jerome Davis pose with a Chinese friend in Peking. Below, Scott and I with a friend in Sweden in July, 1973, when Scott spoke to the International Vegetarian Union Conference.

In April of 1973, Scott was given the title of Honorary Emeritus Professor of Economics at the Wharton School of the University of Pennsylvania. Above, Scott accepts congratulations from the University's President, Martin Meyerson, and the Chairman of the trustees, William L. Day. This honor came 58 years after Scott, then an assistant professor of Economics, was summarily dismissed from the same university because of his public opposition to child labor.

University of Pennsylvania

In recognition of a singular career begun as a member of the Faculty of The Wharton School and for adhering to the belief that to seek out and to teach the truth is life's highest aim the Trustees have designated

Scott Nearing

Honorary Emeritus Professor of Economics effective April 13, 1973

Presented with the sincere appreciation and felicitations of the Trustees, the Faculties, and the Officers of the Corporation this 25th day of April in the year of our Lord one thousand nine hundred and seventy-three and in the year of the University the two hundred and thirty-third.

William L. Day
Chairman of the Trustees

Martin Meyerson
President

William G. Owen
Secretary

91

Scott photographed in Colombo, Ceylon in January, 1968.

Lotte Jacobi

Here I am, knitting, with Scott in the background, at World Fellowship Camp in Conway, New Hampshire in August, 1968. Opposite, Scott and I listen to a young student violinist at a school in Budapest in February, 1968.

92

Above, J.N. Mankar, head of the Indian Humanitarian League, and I admire Scott on a visit to Delhi in November of 1967. Below, Scott (looking like Henry Wallace) converses with Dr. Zakir Husain, then President of India, on the same visit to Delhi, while I listen (looking just like Pearl Buck).

Scott and I in Kyoto, Japan in 1957.

We both attend a meeting at Baku University, USSR in 1957.

Scott addresses a meeting of Jains in Delhi in 1957, with me inattentive.

At the Bombay airport in February of 1957, we are decorated with flowers and photographed with J.N. Mankar.

Above, Scott and I converse with students in Bangalore, India in 1951. Opposite, Scott dons an apron to demonstrate maple sugar cooking in New York in 1950.

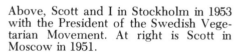

Above, Scott and I in Stockholm in 1953 with the President of the Swedish Vegetarian Movement. At right is Scott in Moscow in 1951.

At left, I play the flute for Scott and Dr. Robert Anderson at a vegetarian conference in Wisconsin in 1941. At right, I pose with Scott's Russian daughter-in-law, Masha, in the USSR in 1931. Below, Scott and I in Russia in 1931; though it is his third or fourth visit there, it is a first for me.

SCOTT'S EARLY DAYS

A portrait made by Earl Brooks, in Arden, Delaware in 1930.

100   Another portrait of Scott, made in 1928 at the age of 45, at about the time I first met him.

These three news photos record Scott's arrest while speaking from a snowbank in Boston, in 1928, after a Communist Party meeting was locked out of a meeting hall. He was released from custody after quoting the First Amendment to the Constitution.

Above, left, is my favorite snapshot of Scott, taken in Pawling, New York about 1929. Above, right; Scott in 1924 in Ridgewood, New Jersey. Opposite is a portrait taken in 1920 before I met him, alas.

At left is Scott with his two sons, Bob and John, in May of 1916. Below is Scott in 1915 posing for the sculptor, Louis Mayer. The bust that resulted is to the right.

Above, in front of the house he built in Arden, Delaware, is Scott in 1914 with his first wife, Nellie Seeds, and Professor Frank Watson of the University of Pennsylvania. At right, Scott wheels his son John by the cornfield in Ridgewood, New Jersey.

Scott, at the far left, with (from left to right) his sisters Mary and Dorothy, brother Guy, sister Beatrice, and brother Max, taken in 1905.

Scott, as a college
freshman, in 1901.

MY EARLY DAYS

Musing in Vienna in 1930.

At right, a 1925 snapshot taken in Australia. Opposite, I am sailing around Orcas Island in the state of Washington in 1928.

Above, I wear Dutch *klompen* (wooden shoes) at the Star Camp in Ommen, Holland in 1930. At right, a 1928 passport picture taken in Holland.

Opposite, above, I am visible in the foreground at the far left. The event was the commemoration of a Buddhist Temple in Adyar, Madras, India in 1925. Below, I am in the highlands of Australia with my ever-present knitting and two Dutch friends, Philip van Pallandt and Juul van Regteren Altena. Above, a 1924 scene in Ommen, Holland. I am behind the wheel of Baron van Pallandt's car, with Mary Lutyens beside me, while Elizabeth Lutyens and Lady Emily, their mother, sit in the back seat. On the running board are Krishnamurti and his brother, Nityananda.

Three photos of me taken in 1922-23. At left, a portrait taken while a violin student in Vienna; at right, a snapshot taken by Krishnamurti at Villa Sonnblick, Ehrwald, in the Austrian Tirol; below, in my room on Amsteldyk, Amsterdam, during my student days.

At right, in 1922, I meditate in Amsterdam at the Theosophical Headquarters. Below, left, I pose mischievously with Krishnamurti in 1921. Below, right, I appear in the 1921 commencement issue of *The Arrow*, Ridgewood High School, New Jersey.

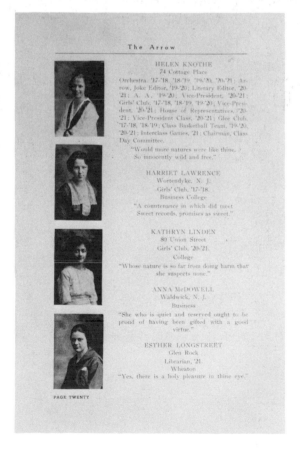

The Arrow

HELEN KNOTHE
74 Cottage Place
Orchestra, '17-'18, '18-'19, '19-'20, '20-'21; Arrow, Joke Editor, '19-'20; Literary Editor, '20-'21; A. A., '19-'20; Vice-President, '20-'21; Girls' Club, '17-'18, '18-'19, '19-'20, Vice-President, '20-'21; House of Representatives, '20-'21; Vice-President Class, '20-'21; Glee Club, '17-'18, '18-'19; Class Basketball Team, '19-'20, '20-'21; Interclass Games, '21; Chairman, Class Day Committee.
"Would more natures were like thine,
So innocently wild and free."

HARRIET LAWRENCE
Wortendyke, N. J.
Girls' Club, '17-'18.
Business College
"A countenance in which did meet
Sweet records, promises as sweet."

KATHRYN LINDEN
80 Union Street
Girls' Club, '20-'21.
College
"Whose nature is so far from doing harm that
she suspects none."

ANNA McDOWELL
Waldwick, N. J.
Business
"She who is quiet and reserved ought to be
proud of having been gifted with a good
virtue."

ESTHER LONGSTREET
Glen Rock
Librarian, '21.
Wheaton
"Yes, there is a holy pleasure in thine eye."

PAGE TWENTY

115

"The Bungalow," as it was called; my home in Ridgewood, New Jersey where I lived during my school years and up to the period of my travels abroad.

AS CHILDREN

Above, left, in 1915 at the age of 12, I hug a beloved cat. At right, a shy Scott, in 1892 at the age of 9, is less demonstrative.

The Nearing family in 1892, at home and afloat. Scott is at the far right in the upper photograph and in the bow of the boat below.

At right, I pose at the age of 7 (on the right) with my mother, Maria Knothe, sister Alice, and brother Alex.

Overleaf; Scott's birthplace in Morris Run, Pennsylvania. From left to right, Louis Nearing, his father; his Aunt Maud; himself; his grandfather, Winfield Scott Nearing (for whom Scott was named); his infant sister, Mary; and his mother, Minnie Zabriskie Nearing.

Opposite, a formal portrait of my family, including my father, Frank, in 1908 when I was four years old; while at right, I am two. Below is Scott at the age of four in 1887, in a gaudy get-up.

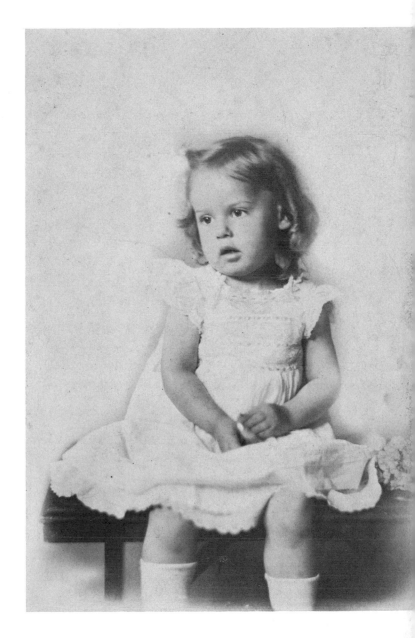

Above, sometime after my first birthday, happily expressing myself. Opposite is Scott in December 1883, four months old, looking like a chick fresh from the egg.

Lotte Jacobi

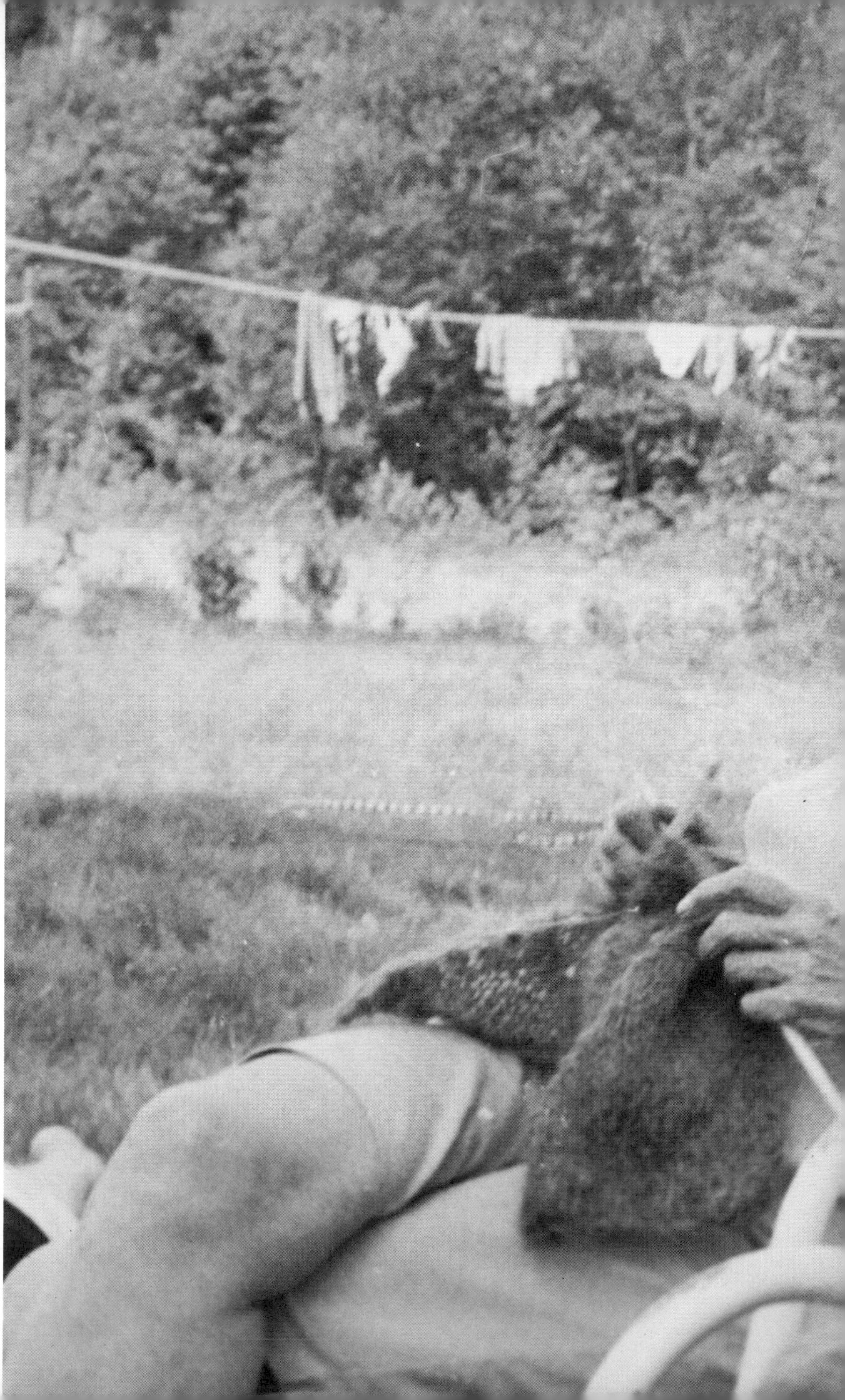